THE SIMPLE THINGS OF THE CHRISTIAN LIFE

The Simple Things

OF THE

Christian Life

BY

G. CAMPBELL MORGAN, D. D.

BAKER BOOK HOUSE
Grand Rapids, Michigan

Paperback edition issued 1976
by Baker Book House Company

ISBN: 0-8010-6000-1

Printed in the United States of America

To

MY STAFF

AT WESTMINSTER

WHO BY PRAYER AND LOVE EVER HELP ME

TO PREACH

CONTENTS

I.   The New Birth 9

II.   Holiness 32

III.   Growth 54

IV.   Work 78

V.   Temptation 101

I

THE NEW BIRTH

"That which is born of the flesh is flesh, and that which is born of the Spirit is spirit."—JOHN iii. 6.

THERE are two facts concerning Christianity which are never called in question at the present hour. The first is, that in the Person of Christ Christianity has revealed to the world the highest ideal of human life it has ever seen. The second is, that in the teaching of Christ Christianity has given to the world at once the most perfect and severest ethical code which has ever been enunciated in the listening ear of humanity. In Him is a perfect Pattern: by Him a perfect law.

Whatever opinion men may hold concerning the principles of Christ, or the doctrines of the Catholic Church, they at least agree that if only all men could live His life, or could perfectly obey His instructions, there would be an immediate solution of all problems, a healing of all wounds, a righting of all wrongs, and the bringing in of that golden age concerning which the prophets and seers and psalmists have been singing to men through all human history. But there is the *if*. *If* men could live as He lived! *If* men could obey His law! And the *if* at once suggests the very solemn and almost appalling consideration that, if Jesus has done no more for men than to have given them the pattern of His life and the illumination of His teaching, He has only succeeded in revealing the depth of human degradation, and the impossibility of man's ever attaining the highest or the best.

I am particularly anxious to state these things as clearly as in me lies, and therefore let me make that last assertion again in slightly different form. If Jesus Christ has done no more than give me the pattern of His life, He has made me the most hopeless and despairing of men, for I cannot reproduce it in my own.

If Jesus Christ has done no more than enunciate the laws which I find in the New Testament records, then He has only succeeded in mocking my impotence, and leaving me helpless and undone upon life's broad highway. I cannot imitate that example, I cannot obey that law, unless He is more than Pattern, more than Law-giver. Unless, in some way, He brings to me the power with the pattern, the dynamic with the ethic, I am hopeless and helpless. The vision of the ideal fills me with great desire, but with an agony of disappointment, for I am brought no nearer to its realisation.

All this is but to say that the very essence of Christianity lies in the fact of the something else that every man demands when he sees the perfect pattern and hears the perfect law. Christianity is not merely an ideal presented. It is not merely a law enunciated. It is essentially a life communicated, in the illumination of which I see perfectly the ideal, and feel all the severity of its demands upon me, and in the power of which I find myself—oh, matchless miracle of grace—being transformed into that fair likeness.

How does this life begin? The third chapter of John is peculiarly interesting and valuable, because it plainly declares the truths concerning the beginning of the Christian life. It also distinctly reveals to us the fact that there were truths which could not be so declared. I find the great principle of the Old Testament manifesting itself very remarkably. "Revealed things" are for us and our children. The "secret things" belong unto God. When Nicodemus, the honest inquirer, looked into the face of his Teacher, and said, *"How* can these things be?" Jesus said to him: "Art thou a teacher of Israel, and understandest not these things? Verily, verily, I say unto thee, we speak that we do know, and bear witness of that we have seen; and ye receive not our witness. If I told you earthly things, and ye believe not, how shall ye believe if I tell you heavenly things?" Christ never attempted to tell the heavenly thing, to unveil the mystery of the life-giving touch of

God. He very clearly stated, however, its conditions of operation. Here, as in all matters where man has to do with forces that are beyond his analysis, He declared the law, obedience to which would place the force at his disposal. He did not explain the force. He did not deal with the infinite mystery, that is for ever more hidden, of God's method of working.

At the heart of this wonderful conversation of Jesus with Nicodemus, the words of my text occur. I have selected these words, not that they form a complete statement within themselves, but because in them Christ explains His insistence upon the necessity for the new birth; and because in them, also, He suggests to us what is the actual nature of the new life to which He is calling men.

Wherein lies the necessity for the new birth? Because "that which is born of the flesh is flesh." What is the nature of the life into which men enter by the new birth? "That which is born of the Spirit is spirit." In this verse we have suggested to us—first, the necessity for, and, secondly, the nature of the new birth.

Let us begin, then, with those words of Jesus, "that which is born of the flesh is flesh." Here we must be careful that we do not read any of our own philosophy into this word of Christ. We must interpret the saying of Christ by Christ Himself, and by His presence and mission. He did not for one moment mean to declare that flesh is in itself necessarily evil. He was not discussing or making reference to any of the philosophies of His own day, which declared the evil nature of the flesh. He was stating a common fact about human nature, dealing with it, as He always did, with reference to its failure and not to its attainment. In His great declarations, "The Son of Man came to seek and to save that which was lost," and "I came not to call the righteous but sinners," He revealed the fact of humanity's helpless and hopeless condition; and He here puts all that fact into the one pregnant sentence, "That which is born of the flesh is flesh."

If I would have that saying of Jesus resolved into its component parts, if I would have it explained satisfactorily to my own mind, I must wait, as the disciples had to wait, for the coming of the Spirit, and for the Spirit's interpretation of the thinking and teaching of Jesus as we have it in the writings of the apostles. Jesus told His disciples distinctly that He had many things to tell them, but they could not bear them then; but when the Comforter should come, He would bring to their remembrance the things that He (Jesus) had said. The office of the Spirit is to unveil the essential, unified truth which Christ uttered, and make it clear, and simple, and plain.

When I turn to the apostolic writings, I find this statement of Jesus elaborated in such a way as to explain to me all that He meant when He said "that which is born of the flesh is flesh." He revealed the fact that man was darkened in his intelligence, alienated in his affection; that he was centring his whole thought upon earthly things; that he was under

the control of the forces of evil. He said in
effect that man lacked spiritual enlightenment,
spiritual appreciation, spiritual aspiration, spiritual freedom; that man did not know God, did
not love God, did not desire God, and did not
serve God. Man, as Christ found him, was altogether satisfied within his own personality.
He had shut the eastern windows through
which the light should stream; he had closed
his ears to the voices that were calling him
from without, and was living entirely within
the realm of the flesh—flesh-centred, flesh-gov-
erned, flesh-mastered.

When Paul begins to break up the truth for
us, he speaks of the carnal mind that cannot
know the things of God; the mind that is at
enmity against God; the mind that has its
affections set upon things of the earth—that is,
under the dominion of the devil. This was
Christ's estimate of humanity without any reference to its cause or permission; and Christ
declares in one all-comprehensive sentence that
man cannot enter into the Kingdom of God

as he is, for "that which is born of the flesh is flesh."

In this word, then, is revealed the necessity for the new birth. A man may see the fair vision of Christ's perfect ideal, but if he be honest he must acknowledge that, when he would do good, evil is present with him; that, when he would realise that high purpose, he finds within him a paralysis that checks endeavour and induces failure. This is the universal experience of human nature of every age and civilisation. In the very fact of man's being, he is of the earth, earthy.

Man does not know God, and no man by searching can find Him out. No man has seen God at any time. No man has conceived the truth about God until he has been born from above. All the wisdom, and culture, and learning of the world and of the successive ages have absolutely failed in their attempt to know God. There are men who know a great deal about God, but they do not know *Him*. Jesus did not say to men that a grasp of theology, a knowledge of the systematised truth concerning God, would bring them life eternal. He said, "This is life eternal to know *God*." No man knows God by his first birth, and because of his ignorance he is at enmity against God. You may challenge that statement. You may tell me this is not the age in which man is at enmity against God. Think well before you make the assertion. Are you welcome in any merely social circle if you want to talk about God? I omit from any such question the circle of Christian people, and yet, even in such, conversation about God is not particularly popular. But go without, not to the vulgar, but to the cultured and refined, and you will find that men do not want to talk of God, nor to think of God. They do not love Him because they do not know Him. If they knew Him they would love Him, and they would talk of Him from early morn till dewy eve. There would be no subject so precious to them as that of God, His Being, and His beneficence. But men do not know Him. They have lost the vision, and there is no affection in the soul for God. Men do not want God; they keep Him out.

What is the issue? The man who has lost the knowledge of God, or who has never had it, and therefore does not love God, turns to the earth, and attempts to feed his soul on dust. The philosophy of the man without God may be expressed in a very few, brief, burning words from Scripture: "What shall we eat? What shall we drink? Wherewithal shall we be clothed?" This is the sum and substance of the life of the soul that does not know God. "Let us eat and drink . . . for to-morrow we die." Was there ever such a pessimistic wail? But it is the honest expression of the man who does not know God. "That which is born of the flesh is flesh." It has lost its vision of God, has no love for God; and it turns to satisfy the clamant cry of its inner life with the things of the earth. It yields, therefore, no allegiance to the throne of high Heaven. It does not ask to know the will of God, and it becomes, all unconsciously, and yet most truly, the slave of its own lust, its own passion, its own animalism; and, finally, therefore, the slave of the devil who drives. These things have not changed with the passing of the years, and this is why man needs to be born anew. "That which is born of the flesh" cannot find God, does not know Him, will not serve Him; and all the surging agony of the world, and its vain cry for satisfaction, finds here its explanation.

Notice in the next place what the Master says: "That which is born of the Spirit is spirit," interpreting what He means in the light of what we have already learned. In the man who is born from above, upon whom this gift of life has been bestowed, a great change is manifested. His life is no longer the flesh life, circumferenced in flesh, centred in flesh. His life is now the spirit life, centred in the spirit, conditioned by the spirit. The man of flesh does not know God. The man born of the Spirit is the friend of God. Give the twenty-third Psalm to a man of scholarship, of refinement, of mental culture at its best. He will return you an exposition full of charm and beauty, in which there will be no false quantity; no mistake about the Eastern shepherd, no wrong view of the still waters of the river, no inaccurate description of the verdure through which the sheep are led. It will be poetic, finished, a thing of beauty, but a stone which cannot feed the soul. Give that same twenty-third Psalm to some old mother in Israel, who never could read it, but has learned it. Ask her to recite it, and tell you her experience of it; and you know as well as I do that the windows of Heaven are open, and—

> "God comes down the soul to greet,
>   While glory crowns the mercy-seat."

The man is living in the flesh, and though he approaches the Divine thing, he never touches it. The woman lives in the spirit, and although she speaks in ungrammatical language, and violates its metaphors, and misinterprets its illustrations, she yet unveils the heart of God.

The man lives in the flesh: it may be refined and cultured, but devoid of spiritual vision. The soul that has come into the spirit realm sees and talks about the things invisible, touches and talks about the things intangible. The man smiles at her folly, and pities her; but she is seeing God!

Have you ever seen God, my brother, my sister? Your truthful answer will reveal whether you are born again or not. If you have not seen Him, if you have only imagined Him, if you are still speculating as to His existence, you do not know anything about the new birth. If you have seen Him with the vision that is not fleshly, if you know Him, then life is yours. That which is born of the Spirit takes hold of the Spirit, appreciates the Spirit; it knows God. That is the first thing.

The second is that it loves God. There are men and women everywhere who love God. The mention of His name stirs the heart as nothing else can. The thought of His infinite **grace** and matchless love brings tears when nothing else will bring them, and provokes a smile that lights the dreariest day the soul ever passed through. The knowledge of God is always the birth of love in the soul. You cannot know God and not love Him. To know Him is to love Him. I am never tired of quoting the words of a German poet, who sang:

> " O God, of good the unfathomed sea;
> Who would not give his heart to Thee?"

That was the language of a man who had seen God. When he had seen Him, and had come to know Him, he handed over everything he had to Him. He did what love always does— became prodigal in his giving, poured himself out—heart, will, mind, and devotion. That is always the answer when a man sees God. "That which is born of the Spirit is spirit."

The man born of the Spirit holds with a loose hand the things of the world. Not that he is careless about flowers. He loves them because they are sacramental symbols of the infinite touch of his Father. He is not careless of the birds.   He loves them because they sound in his listening ear tones of the music of the Father's home.   He is not careless of the old world.   He loves it, but always because he sees through its beauties the God he has come to love.   He does not try to satisfy his soul with the things of to-day.   He is not concerned with what he shall eat, and what he shall drink, and wherewithal he shall be clothed.   His first and supreme concern is the Kingdom of God and His righteousness, and he knows that his material wants will be supplied.   These things often are, after all, but the baggage which threatens to retard the progress, the impedimenta which man will let fall as he drops the robe of flesh, and, rising into his native air, has personal and everlasting vision of God, and communion with Him.

The final distinction of the man who sees and loves God, who knows and obeys Him, lies in the principle that now governs his life. His motives and aims are no longer selfish and worldly, his actions no longer constrained by fleshly desires. Henceforth he recognises the right of one "must" alone, and that the impelling obligation of the will of God.

No man can pass into this new spirit life out of the old flesh life save by the touch of the Spirit upon him, and by communication of the Spirit life to him. Does the necessity attract us? Does it appal us? Is someone looking on the spiritual side, and saying how he would fain enter into that life? Or is someone looking on the fleshly side. Is your question that of Nicodemus: "*How* can these things be?" Then comes the Master's answer, with characteristic limitation, and yet with wonderful clearness. Let us consider that answer, taking first His statement of the mystery of the new birth; and, secondly, His declaration regarding the law of its operation.

First, then, how does Jesus answer the universal question, as voiced by Nicodemus? "The wind bloweth where it listeth, and thou hearest the voice thereof, but knowest not whence it cometh and whither it goeth. So is everyone that is born of the Spirit." In that statement there is a recognition of mystery, and a recognition of principle. "The wind bloweth where it listeth . . . so is everyone that is born of the Spirit." What does that "so" refer to? To the wind? No. Our relation to the wind expresses the relation of man to the Spirit. We must have our balances right here, or we shall never understand this great verse. We hear the wind; this man hears the voice of the Spirit. We cannot tell whence the wind comes, nor whither it goes; this man cannot explain the mystery of the Spirit's guidance. Christ leaves it there. It is the commencement of an illustration which He left Nicodemus to work out for himself. What is the natural outworking of it? I hear the sound of the wind—that is the fact. I cannot tell whence it cometh nor whither it goeth—that is the mystery. What follows? I take hold of the fact and obey its law, and I gain the benefit, even though I do not understand the mystery.

Some of you know something about boating. You put your boat upon the lake, and hoist your sail, and wait for the wind. Now it is blowing—that is a fact. You do not know whence it comes, nor whither it goes—that is a mystery. But you do not sit down in the boat and say, I decline to make any use of this thing. I do not understand it. I cannot be swayed by mystery. I must have an explanation. Nonsense! You put your sail up, saying, I will take advantage of the fact in order that my boat may be driven over the lake, and postpone the solution of the mystery to further knowledge and understanding. So much for the man and the wind. "So is everyone that is born of the Spirit." You know the fact of the Spirit. You do not know the mystery of His coming and going.

What then shall I do? Discover the law and obey it? Though I cannot explain the mystery of the new birth, I shall receive the benefit of the Spirit's power, and shall get the life. But what is the law? "As Moses lifted up the serpent in the wilderness, even so must the Son of man be lifted up: that whosoever believeth, may in Him have eternal life." Here is the law! Life comes by the Spirit when you believe on the lifted Son of man. Talking to Nicodemus, those wondrous eyes looked on to the bloody Cross, and with calm, heroic fortitude, Jesus said: "The Son of man must be lifted up." You ask me how you can get life. He that believeth on the Son shall have life. Life will come to the soul through that lifting up. Again a mystery without explanation; but there is the fact and its law. The Spirit will communicate to the soul who believes the life liberated in the mystery of the Passion. Are you asking how? Never mind the how! Hoist your sail, and catch the breeze of this Spirit of God! Obey the law while you postpone the explanation of the mystery. Obey the law, and that Spirit Whose coming and going no man can perfectly understand, will communicate to your soul at this moment the very life of that perfect One, Who was the ideal and Whose was the ethic; and that life communicated will become the dynamic, in the power of which you will realise the pattern and walk in obedience to His commands.

How am I to be born again? Recognise the mystery of the Spirit's work. Discover the law of the Spirit's operation. Obey the law, and immediately receive the benefit. Just as the man upon the lake, who, not understanding the mystery of the coming and going of the wind, yet obeys its law by lifting his sail so as to catch it, and finds his boat driven across the water; so you, helpless man, unable to understand the mystery of the Incarnation, or of Atonement, or of regeneration, lift your sail, crown Christ by trusting Him, and the Divine afflatus shall fill your soul. You will begin the voyage that ends in endless life beyond the mysteries and mists of the "little while." It is a great mystery! I do not know how I was born again. I do not know how God changed this fleshly life of mine into one that sees something of His beauty, and loves

Him a little already. I do not know how He wrought the change, and made me love the thing I hated, and hate the thing I loved. He did it when I believed on Jesus, and as I obeyed that simple law which Christ Himself declared, I was born again, and began a life as different from the old as noonday is different from midnight, as the grapes of Eshcol from the apples of Sodom.

Oh, begin this life; begin right where you are, without a sign or sound, without word spoken to friend or neighbour. Close the eyes of your soul, and say, O Christ, Revealer of God, Redeemer of men, by the mystery of the Passion that I cannot understand, in obedience to the call of Thy love, I trust Thee with my soul.

There will be no newspaper paragraph. There are some things the newspapers cannot describe; but it will be recorded in heaven, and you will pass from death to life, from the thraldom of the world to the liberty of the child of God. God help us to see that there is mystery that cannot be explained, though there is also a law that is simple enough for a child; and that when we obey the law, all the forces of God's life in Christ are made ours by the work of the Spirit.

II

HOLINESS

"Like as He which called you is holy, be ye yourselves also holy in all manner of living; because it is written, Ye shall be holy; for I am holy."—1 PETER i. 15, 16.

THIS text is a somewhat startling one. Indeed, it is so startling that it has in very many cases ceased to startle. Men have read it, and have been surprised, and then, withdrawing from its call and claim, have treated it for ever afterwards as though it did not mean what it said. That is the kind of Bible criticism of which I am afraid. The criticism of the spirit of accommodation which attempts to lower the Bible standard is most perilous.

I can well understand that a text like this should startle, even affright, the unregenerate man. To hear the word which declares that without holiness no man shall see God must surely be to fill his heart with terror. He knows full well that however much he may admire the ideal of holiness, he is utterly unable to realise that ideal in his own life and experience.

But if this be true, let me hasten to add that to the child of God a call like this should certainly bring no terror. Searching of heart, yes; earnestness of endeavour to apprehend its meaning, certainly; consecrated abandonment toward the purpose indicated, absolutely; but fear, terror, certainly not!

And yet how many Christian people there are who are afraid of the very word "holy," of the term "holiness." I am not at all sure that it is altogether their fault. I am painfully conscious that some very unholy things have been done in the name of holiness. I know that some things which lack the reality of sanctity have gathered about them its odour. I am not at all surprised that some people are afraid of the term, even though they are children of God. Yet it is not quite fair to turn away from so palpable and evident a purpose of God for our life because the reality has been travestied.

My present desire is to deal with the way of holiness so as to be helpful to two classes of persons. First, to those who have experienced the new birth, and to God's own children who are yet conscious of failure, conscious still of very much in their daily life that is unlike their Lord, who nevertheless earnestly desire to live the life which is holy. I also want to speak of the subject to many who are on the border-line of decision, who have been attracted toward Christ because of the beauty of His character, and who are asking, ere they set their feet in the way of His commandments, whether it will be possible for them to live the life to which He calls them.

How many such there are. I say without reservation that no week passes in which I am not brought personally or by correspondence into contact with earnestly sincere souls who are outside the Kingdom, yet wishing to be inside; who tarry because they are afraid lest, having turned their faces toward the King, and yielded to Him, they should dishonour His name. I have a profound respect for such fear, but I do not think it is warranted. I think they need tarry no longer doubting and trembling outside, and yet my heart always goes out to the man who looks into my eyes and says, I would like to be a Christian, but I am afraid I should not be worthy of the name.

I wish to speak to you of this holy way, this holy life that follows, and never precedes the new birth, in order that you may be helped to decision, as you see not only what holiness is, but what the power for it is; and, moreover, what your responsibility concerning it will be when you become a child of God.

First of all, by way of definition, what is holiness? It is an interesting fact that this word, with which we are all so familiar, which lies so constantly upon the pages of our Bibles in the Old and New Testaments, occurring in differing forms hundreds of times in both sections of the Divine Library, has no exact equivalent in the original language in either the Old or New Testament. I do not mean to say that the idea it suggests is any different from that suggested by the Bible terms. I think the word is right wherever you find it. Yet it is interesting in attempting to understand what Scripture means by the terms it makes use of, to get beneath the words we use to the primitive meaning of the words of which they are a translation. In the Old Testament the word "holiness," and all cognate words, are almost invariably derived from a Hebrew word which suggests sanctity—that is, the separation or setting apart of the thing described as sacred to the purposes of God alone. All the vessels of the ancient sanctuary were holy, but the thought of the word is that they were set apart to the Divine use and the Divine purpose. That is the first use of this word, or rather of the word we have translated "holy" in the Scriptures of truth. So that a word meaning separated, set apart, is used to indicate the necessary condition of cleanness in the thing so set apart.

In a moment the mind sees the reasonableness of the word. Said one of the prophets, understanding that fact, "Be ye clean, ye that bear the vessels of the Lord." The men who were to handle the holy separated vessels were themselves to be holy, separated, and their holiness and separation were to have as a quality, cleanness of life.

When I turn to the New Testament I find another word behind the word "holiness" and "sanctification"; a word which, from the standpoint of etymology, is not the same as the Hebrew word, although in use it means exactly the same thing. The word of the New Testament is one which signifies something that is awful, full of awe. The holy thing is one which produces a feeling of awe in the soul of the man who comes into contact with it. Holiness is a condition awe-inspiring. To leave the statement there would be utterly to misinterpret the use of the word in the New Testa-

ment. Why are things awful which are holy?
Why are things which have the quality we
have translated holiness, awe-inspiring? They
are awful things because separated to God,
belonging peculiarly and only to Him. That
is the thought of the word wherever you find
it in the New Testament. All that belonged
to God inspired awe in the soul simply because it was His, separated to His use, set apart
exclusively to Him. So the word used to indicate the condition of life which fitted men for
separation to God was a word which indicated
the awe inspired in the heart by the fact of
separation.

For a moment let us tarry there. Separation to God is after all what holiness means.
The difference between the regenerate man and
the unregenerate man is the difference between the man who belongs to God and the
man who is at the disposal of any and every
master who pays his price. I do not think this
thing can be put more forcefully than by a
simple illustration. The difference essentially

between the regenerate man and the unregenerate man is the difference between Buckingham Palace and the Hotel Cecil. The Hotel Cecil, or any other hotel, is at the disposal of any man who can pay enough to hire it, but no one can hire Buckingham Palace. That is the dwelling-place of the king. Lust can hire the hotel, benevolence can hire the hotel for its annual dinner, anyone can hire the hotel who pays the price; but you cannot hire Buckingham Palace. No millionaire can hire it. Thank God there is something they cannot do! I have tried to make the illustration simple, that the truth in all its sublimity may break upon our consciousness. Here are two men. One of them is an unregenerate man. The other is born anew. The unregenerate man can be bought. I do not mean that any other man can buy him, but he will hire himself out to whatever pays the price he demands. Lust, avarice, drunkenness, debauchery, beneficence, philanthropy, anything that will give him his price, to it he will hand over his life. The regenerate man, if he understand the meaning of his regeneration, nothing can buy. He is the sanctuary, the temple, the dwelling-place of God. New Testament writers describe him as awe-inspiring, for such is a man who inspires other men with reverence and wonder as they recognise in him the peculiar, personal property of God.

Holiness, then, is that which inspires awe, because it indicates the separation of a soul to God. Such is the meaning of the word, and although from the standpoint of etymology our word "holiness" has no relation to either of the two thoughts expressed, yet there is in the use of it a strange and wonderful fitness. Long ago, all unconsciously, perhaps, the Christian Church fastened upon the word "holy" in order to express the condition of the man separated to God, and inspiring awe by that separation.

What, then, does our word "holiness" mean? It may be traced to a simple Anglo-Saxon root, *halig,* which means whole—complete. From that root two words have come into common use, namely, health and holiness. In our differentiation in the use of words which have originally the same meaning, we have applied the word *health* to things physical, and the word *holiness* to things spiritual. We talk of a man as having a healthy body, or as being of a holy spirit, and we express exactly the same thing in differing spheres by the distinguishing adjectives which we use. I should do no violence to the intention if I spoke of a man with a holy body and a healthy spirit. In other words, what health is to the body, holiness is to the spirit; and taken in its simplicity, holiness means health, wholeness, perfection in the spiritual sphere.

It follows, then, that there can be no holiness apart from life, for the very use of the word *health* implies a pre-existing life principle. Given the life, then, holiness is simply that life maintained in health before God. This definition saves our word from abuse, for through it we see that holiness is not perfection of consummation, but only perfection of condition. An illustration will perhaps throw light upon my meaning. In winter time we look upon a tree which is stripped of all its leaves. One spring morning we discover a bud full of promise, and we exclaim at its perfection. But what is the perfection of the bud? Is it the perfection of consummation? You would be very sorry if that were so, if it remained a bud through all the months; and yet it has a perfection, the perfection of condition. It is healthy and sound, perfect in potentiality. Let the weeks pass on, and let us visit the tree once again. A blossom has taken the place of the bud; and we again marvel at the perfection of its beauty. A little later, and the bud has found its final perfection in the rich, ripe, luscious fruit upon the tree. It is now perfect, not only as to condition, but as to consummation; not only in potentiality, but in realisation. But the health, the wholeness is no more perfect in the fruit than it was in the bud or the blossom.

There is the same quality of holiness in every stage.

To illustrate again on a higher plane. Come with me into some home, and look at that baby in its mother's arms. Is it perfect? Ask the mother! Is that the perfection of consummation? That mother's heart would break if the child remained at that stage as the years passed on, and there were no advance and no development; but it is perfect in condition, in health. The years pass on, and I bring you again to that home. The babe is no longer a babe, but a boy of sixteen or seventeen years of age. I show you the boy with the light of health upon his brow, the aspiration of young manhood beginning to burn in his eye. Is that perfection? Yes, in condition, in possibilities, but not in development. The perfection of consummation will only come with the years, and the burden, and passion, and testing fire; and yet there is a perfection all the way through.

I turn to Philippians, and in Paul's great

autobiographical chapter I read: "Not that I have already obtained, or am already made perfect"; and within a very few sentences he says: "Let us, therefore, as many as be perfect." What does he mean? In one sentence he says that he is not perfect, and in another he says, in effect, that he is perfect. It is the difference between the perfection of consummation and the perfection of condition. I am not yet perfected. I have not yet obtained, not yet apprehended, not yet reached the goal. The final crown is not yet upon my brow. The last glory has not yet dawned upon my soul. And yet I am perfect in my attitude, in my running in the heavenward trend of my affections and will. "One thing I do— I press toward the goal." So when I go back to the garden, and look at the bud, it says to me, I have not yet attained, but one thing I do—I press on. I come to the blossom, and it says to me, I have not yet apprehended that which I signify, and toward which I live. One thing I do, forgetting the limited perfection of the bud, I press in throbbing life toward the ultimate fruitage. In that *one thing* with all its underlying meaning, is the health of the bud and blossom.

And so we cannot have the perfection of consummation. We cannot yet apprehend all that is ours in Jesus Christ, but we can be holy. We can in our own spiritual life be all that is possible to us at the moment. Growth there must be, development there will be, and it may be a long, rough journey before we reach the mountain height, and know what perfection means. We shall never know the perfection of consummation until the second advent. Then, and not till then, will He "fashion anew the body of our humiliation, that it may be conformed to the body of His glory." That is the perfection of consummation, but, here and now, you and I can have the perfection of condition, of spiritual health, of holiness.

If this be true, what is the power for holiness? How can I be holy, healthy, in my spiritual life? The answer is that holiness consists, as to dynamic, in the life which I receive in my new birth. If I will answer that life, and will let that life have its way, it will maintain itself in health. Real life never needs the administration of anything from without save proper food, and proper air, and proper exercise. Anything that quickens life unnaturally, leaves it more lifeless presently. The man who takes into the fibre of his physical life, alcohol, pure oxygen, or anything else to artificially quicken, kills while he does it. So with the spiritual life. If you have been born again, you have received life with all the potentialities of holy living. Answer its call.

Let us state that principle in another way. There is a great word in that same Philippian epistle, "Work out your own salvation with fear and trembling." What an endless pity it is that we so often quote that text, and leave it there. That is the ethic without the dynamic. This is what the apostle wrote: "Work out your own salvation with fear and trembling;

for it is God which worketh in you both to will
and to work, for His good pleasure." What
is that life that came to you when you yielded
yourself to Christ? The life of God. You
were made partaker of the Divine nature. In
that moment, by processes that we cannot
finally explain, when you obeyed the call of
the Spirit by yielding yourself to Christ, the
Spirit communicated to you the life of God.
Answer it, let it dominate; do not check it,
curtail it, stifle it. God is working in you,
and, mark the words, He works in you "to
will and to work," to create desire, and to
supply energy which turns desire into realisation and achievement. "It is God which
worketh in you." I wish I could put this
truth as I feel it. Holiness does not depend
upon your effort at all. Holiness simply depends upon your abandoning yourself to the
indwelling Spirit of God, that He may maintain in health the life which He has Himself
communicated. The power for holiness is not
in the flesh, but in the Spirit. The way in

which man can live the Christ-life in health and strength, and ever-increasing strength, is simply that of answering the call of the life within him.

It is true there are responsibilities. What are they? Briefly stated they include—First, a renunciation of all things of which the life of God disapproves; second, an abandonment of the whole being to God, that He may possess the territory, and realise it according to His will, and for His glory; third, the maintaining of simple quiet trust in Him, which expresses itself in obedience and patient waiting for His guidance.

First, the renunciation of all things which the life of God in the soul condemns. What are these things? I cannot answer that question for another man. It is quite possible for the Christian teacher to indicate the principles by which we may know these things, but the things themselves ought never to be named by one man to another. The things which hinder the life of God in me may not hinder it in you; and the things which hinder the life of God in you may not hinder it in me.

I cannot better declare the principles than by reminding you of the very clear definitions of sin which the New Testament gives. "Sin is lawlessness," or, taking a section of the great meaning as it is in the Authorised Version, "Sin is transgression of the law." Then if a man would answer the life of God within himself, he must resolutely put out of his life the things he knows to be wrong. I cannot live the holy life, I cannot be healthy spiritually, if I am giving shelter in my life, in its habits, in its thinking, in the chamber of the imagination, in the palace of affection, to things I know to be wrong. I must put such things outside.

The second definition of sin is that of James. "To him therefore that knoweth to do good, and doeth it not, to him it is sin." That is a littler subtler than the other, a little more searching. The first declares that to do wrong, the second, that to neglect to do right, is sin. I venture to give an illustration of this principle—James's own illustration—and I take it because I am perfectly sure it is not at all a popular one to-day. "Ye say, To-day, or to-morrow we will go into this city and spend a year there and trade, and get gain . . . ye ought to say, If the Lord will, we shall both live and do this or that . . . to him therefore that knoweth to do good, and doeth it not, to him it is sin." According to James, the Christian man ought not only to say in his heart, "If the Lord will" with regard to his plans, but also with his lips. I know this is an age when such an expression as "God willing" sounds like cant. James says, Wear the label of your loyalty. Use the speech of your surrender. Say, "if the Lord will," as well as mean it. If you know you ought to do this, and neglect it, that is sin. I cannot live the holy life if I am neglecting at any point something that in my inner heart I know I ought to be doing.

Once again, take Paul's definition, which is more searching still. It gets a little deeper, yet is more comforting and helpful than the others.

"Whatsoever is not of faith is sin." "He that doubteth is condemned." Then the man of faith must do nothing upon the basis of doubt. So long as I am doing anything, either that which seems to be right, or that which seems to be wrong, wondering whether I ought to do so, I am sinning. I know that cuts two ways, and it is wonderfully helpful if we can only get hold of it. I am constantly being asked, Do you think I ought to go to the theatre? I will give the answer here which I would give in private: Ask your Master, do not ask me. Propound your question in the presence of Calvary. Look into the very face of the One you call Lord and King, and say, Jesus, may I go to the theatre? Remember, however, that the fact that you are in doubt shows that you ought not to go. "Whatsoever is not of faith is sin." You may take that principle and apply it in another way. For instance, a young man comes to me, and says, I am not at all sure, but I have a sort of idea I ought to enter the Christian ministry. What shall I say to him? I say, For God's sake, and the sake of humanity, keep out! No man who only thinks, and is not sure, should enter the Christian ministry. As long as you are in doubt, stay where you are. This is a principle that works all through. If the life of God is to be maintained in the soul in strength, there must be renunciation, the wrong thing must be put out of the life at all costs. The neglect of right must be remedied. I must do the thing I know I ought to do, even though it means tramping a thorny path with blood tracks all the way. The doubtful thing that I have played with, and wondered about, must be cut off, however wrong, or however right it may seem. I must live upon the principle of simple faith in my Lord and Master, with immediate and ready answer to every demand of His gracious will.

I believe these to be the only conditions of holiness. Let me fulfil them, and let me by such fulfilment honestly hand over my life to His control, and by such fulfilment demonstrate my perfect confidence in Him, and He will perfect that which concerneth me. He will maintain this weak soul of mine in spiritual health, in holiness, in perfection of condition. That is not the last thing. It is the first thing. Holiness is not finality. It is the first condition for development toward finality. Everything is yet to come of growth, advancement, realisation. We pause here. "Be ye holy" is God's call. Say no longer that you cannot be holy. Say, rather, that in the power of His life you can. May God help us to such an attitude.

III

GROWTH

" Ye, therefore, beloved, knowing these things before-hand, beware lest, being carried away with the error of the wicked, ye fall from your own stedfastness. But grow in the grace and knowledge of our Lord and Saviour Jesus Christ. To Him be the glory both now and for ever. Amen."—2 PETER iii. 17, 18.

WE have already defined holiness as health of spiritual life. We were careful to distinguish between perfection of condition, which is holiness, and perfection of consummation, which is the final goal of the holy being. We saw how the youngest disciples of Jesus Christ can be holy, perfect as to condition, but cannot yet be perfect with the perfection of consummation. The disciple who has been following Jesus Christ for years can be holy, but will yet say, and will say to the end of the earthly pilgrimage, "I have not yet apprehended."

But there is a morning coming which will be
without clouds. Then we shall see Him as He
is, and we shall be like Him, and shall be able to
say at last, We have apprehended that for
which we have been apprehended by Christ
Jesus.

While the figure of the bud and the blossom
that we made use of teaches the possibility
of a perfection of condition through all the
processes, with equal force it illustrates the
necessity for growth and development. Health
is not a condition of life beyond which there
can be nothing more. Health is the condition for growth, not a reason for its cessation.
Holiness is not a condition beyond which there
is neither room nor need for development.
Holiness is the necessary condition for development. With that subject of growth and
development I propose now to deal. I want
to deal first with the naturalness of the growth
of the Christian life and character; secondly,
with the direction of such growth; finally, and
principally, with the responsibilities concern-

ing growth which rest upon those of us who have received the life of God, and in whom it is being maintained in health.

First, then, concerning the naturalness of growth. Growth is dependent upon life and health. Grant these conditions, and it follows naturally and without effort. If these be absent there can be no growth. We may use the word sometimes somewhat carelessly in relation to matters which are devoid of life, but, strictly speaking, it always indicates the presence of life. Boys at their play in wintertime will take a small snowball, and, rolling it in the snow, will watch it becoming larger and larger, until one boy says, See how it grows! No, it is not growing. That is not growth. That is enlargement by accretion from without. Growth is enlargement by development from within. The principle of life is necessary to growth. You may challenge the accuracy of that statement as a general one, but I want to point out very carefully and particularly that the word "grow" in the text is always used in that connection in Scripture. The Greek word is translated "grow" or "increase," and it is never used save in the realm of life in some form. For instance, "Consider the lilies of the field, how they grow." "Let both grow together until the harvest." "Your faith groweth." "I planted, Apollos watered; but God gave the increase." "Maketh the increase of the body." The life principle is present whether you think of the lilies, or of the darnel or the wheat, or of the faith of the Christian, or of the development of the whole Church of Jesus Christ. When the apostle Peter charges us in his epistle to "grow in grace" he presupposes the presence of life, and it is of the utmost importance that we emphasise that fact. There can be no growth in Christian character save where the Christ-life exists. The man who is born anew can grow in grace. The man who has not received the gift of life cannot grow. Growth in grace is not the result of the imitation of Christ in the power of the human will.

It is the result of the propelling force of the Christ-life in the soul.

If growth be dependent upon life, it is equally dependent upon health. Arrest of development is always due to disease of some kind. And is not disease itself always due to failure of the life principle to reach some part of the organism? Are not scientists telling us to-day that "the blood is the life"? We who had our Bibles in our hands knew it long ago. Are not scientists affirming to-day, to use their own method of expression so far as I am able, that the blood is the greatest germicide in existence? If the life principle in the body, the blood, can but find its way to all the parts of the body, disease is made impossible thereby. Doctors may differ as to the accuracy of that statement, but whether that theory represents the truth or not in the realm of the material, it certainly does in that of the spiritual. Wherever there is arrest of development in the Christian life it is due to the fact that, in some part of the life, the life principle of Jesus

Christ is not obtaining and dominant. Some part of the life—the intellect, the emotion, the will, the chamber of the imagination, the palace of the affection, or the seat of thought—is not wholly handed over to the indwelling Christ, is not answering the call of His life, is not responding to its claims. The tides of that life are excluded from some part of the being, and the result is spiritual disease. The spiritual faculties become atrophied. They cannot work. Then follows arrest of development. But granted the full rushing tide of the Christ-life in all the departments of the believer's life, granted the presence and dominance of that life in all the complex mystery of his being, then he is in health, and his growth steady and sure.

Growth, therefore, is never the result of effort. I remember, ten years ago, when I first set my face to the other side of the sea, my boy, six years of age, said to me as he bade me good-bye, "How long shall you be away?" I told him two months. He said, "I am going to try hard to grow as big as you are before you come back." I am not sure that he tried. I suspect he forgot, as children do so blessedly forget their follies. But if he did try, he did not succeed. No child grows by effort. No man "by being anxious can add one cubit to his stature." Growth in Christian stature is never the result of effort. I want to say this emphatically for the comfort of some of my brothers and sisters who have recently given themselves to Jesus Christ, and who, perhaps, are a little disappointed that, notwithstanding their earnest striving after a perfect Christian character, they have failed. It is not by your effort that you grow. Granted life and holiness, then there will be growth and development.

In the second place, it is necessary to notice the direction of growth. Let us look at that wonderful fourth chapter of the letter to the Ephesians, and we must beware here, as always in the writings of the apostle, of confusing the main line of his argument with the side issues.

I am not going to attempt an exposition of
the whole passage. It will be enough to ex-
tract from it its principal statement by taking
verse 7, the first two words of verse 14, and
the latter part of verse 15. Everything I miss
out is absolutely important, but it is second-
ary and illustrative. The main declaration of
the whole passage is this, "Unto each one of
us was grace given . . . that we . . . may
grow up in all things into Him, Who is the
head, even Christ."

In that great statement we see what is the
direction of Christian growth. It is growth
into the likeness of Jesus Christ. Where the
life of God is received by a soul, and fully
yielded, that soul is day by day, hour by hour,
yea, moment by moment, growing into the likeness of the Son of God. When presently, by
God's grace, we reach the perfection of consummation, when presently we have done with
the bud of promise and the blossom of hope,
and have come to the fruitage of realisation,
what will that final glory be? The psalmist

of old had a fore-glimpse of it when he said, "I shall be satisfied when I awake with Thy likeness." The apostle John saw it even more clearly, "Beloved, now are we children of God, and it is not yet made manifest what we shall be. We know that if He shall be manifested, we shall be like Him; for we shall see Him even as He is." The consummation of Christian character is perfect approximation to the character of Jesus Christ. We shall have reached the fruitage of Christian life when we see Him, and when we are like Him. Growth into His likeness, then, is the line of Christian development.

But there is another truth—no, not another, rather a complement to the one great truth which is also in the chapter in Ephesians. It is that, as I grow up into His likeness, I grow into my true place in His body, which is the Church. I become fitted to fulfil that special function in the Church's life which is allotted to me by the appointment of Jesus through the Holy Spirit. Thus the double standard by which we may test ourselves perpetually is this : first, am I more like Christ than I was? second, is my union with the Church of Christ such as will help it to become the perfect medium through which the glories of the Head shall be manifest to the ages? Perhaps we had better leave for the present that second half of our consideration, important and vital as it is, and confine ourselves to the first.

The great test question with which the believer should start each day, and with which he should close each day, is this : Am I more like my Lord than I was? This is not a question that a man can ask and answer in *dilettante* fashion, treating it as he would some trifling consideration of the passing hour. It is a question of fire, testing the motives and actions; a question of arraignment, setting the soul daily before a great tribunal. Am I more like Jesus Christ than I was? Who is to answer the question? I am to answer it, not in the public ear, but in the inner shrine of my own spirit, and in the presence of my Lord—to tell Him. I know that the nearer a man gets to Christ, the further away he feels himself to be. That is one of the paradoxes of the Christian life. You follow after Him with all your heart, climbing the mountain at whose summit He awaits you; and the distance appears greater with every approaching step. The man, or woman, or little child, and most probably the little child, who has come nearest to the Christ of God, is most conscious of distance from Him.

Yet for all practical purposes we may know whether we are growing more like Jesus Christ or not. Let me make the question very practical and pertinent by means of a homely illustration. Some years ago, a member of one of my former congregations, a Christian woman of refinement and of great consecration, went to stay in the home of her sister in the country, where she had not stayed for many years. Her sister was a woman of the world, engrossed in worldly pleasures and interests.

When my friend was leaving the home, after a stay of two weeks, her sister, taking her by the hand, and looking into her face, said, "I do not understand your religion, but I will tell you one thing; it has made you far easier to live with." That is your test. Am I easier to live with? Am I more easily entreated, more tender, more compassionate, more ready to forgive? Is there in my life more of the love that "believeth all things, hopeth all things, endureth all things," more of the love—mark this well—that "taketh not account of evil"? That is a very commercial phrase. If you will translate it freely you may render it thus: Love does not keep a ledger in which it enters evil deeds. Have I more of that love? Is my heart more compassionate toward the lost? That is only one side of the test. There is another side. Am I more capable than I was of anger against all forms of sin and iniquity? Am I more daring and courageous than I used to be in my opposition to everything that opposes itself against God? If I am more like Jesus

Christ, I am at once more tender and more severe, more gentle, winsome and winning, and more terrific in my denunciation of evil, and in my battle against it. If I am more like Jesus Christ than I was, sinners turning from sin will seek me out more than they used to do, and sinners persisting in sin will shun me more than they used to do. Am I more like Jesus Christ than I was? Ah me, and alas! for the Christian souls who have to answer No. Alas! for the men and women everywhere who are sighing Cowper's hymn,

> " Where is the blessedness I knew,
> When first I saw the Lord ? "

I am not criticising Cowper for writing it, but my heart is always sorry for the cause of his writing it; and more sorry still for the man who sings it, and imagines the singing of it is a sign of grace. Where is the blessedness you knew when first you saw the Lord? It is where you left it, when you turned your face toward the accursed thing, and became a curse to other people because of your disloyalty. The Christian man should grow into likeness to Christ. Every sorrow should leave behind it some added touch of sanctity, and every joy should bring the blush and bloom of the beauty of holiness; and every day should see some advance toward the realisation of the Christian character. If I have to look back and say that ten years ago I was more like Christ than I am to-day, it is high time I began to search for the reason of the decline. It is high time I discovered the point at which the disease entered, which prevented the dominance of the Christ-life, and paralysed my faculties, and robbed me of my power. There should be growth; and growth into the likeness of Christ.

That leads me to the last point. What are the responsibilities of the Christian concerning growth? While growth is the result of life and health, and never of mere effort, there are positive means of grace which must be carefully observed if the soul would grow into likeness to Christ. Let us turn back to that passage in Ephesians, "To each one of us was grace given," and, keeping that in mind, listen to the words of the text: "Grow in the grace and knowledge of our Lord and Saviour Jesus Christ." The text does not mean, grow into the grace, or into the knowledge. It means exactly what it says, and may be stated in this wise: Being in grace—grow. Being in knowledge of our Lord Jesus Christ—grow. That is clear when we read verse 17 as well as verse 18. "Ye, therefore, beloved, *knowing* these things beforehand, beware lest being carried away with the error of the wicked, ye fall from your own stedfastness. But grow in the grace and knowledge of our Lord and Saviour Jesus Christ." "Beware lest ye fall," that is the negative command. The positive command is, "*Knowing* these things . . . grow in the grace and knowledge." You are in the grace, in the knowledge! Grow! Grace is given to every child of God; grow in it. Knowledge of Jesus is the peculiar fundamental quality of Christian life. No man can call Him Lord but by the Spirit; but when the Spirit comes, He is known as Lord. You know Him, grow in that knowledge. You are in grace, for grace is given to each one in order that we may grow up into Him. Answer the grace in which you dwell. Being in the grace—grow. That is the general statement.

But there is a particular statement. Just now I made use of a phrase which is sometimes misused, I think, the "means of grace." What are the means of grace? If you speak to me of the Christian sacraments or ordinances, I tell you they are but the emblems of the means of grace. The Sacrament of the Lord's Supper is not in itself a means of grace. It is a symbol merely. Baptism in any kind is not a means of grace. It is but an outward sign. What, then, are the means of grace? Simply those laws and regulations which Christ imposed, and which man must observe. Here is the point of our responsibility, and I cannot, I think, better enforce this truth concerning responsibility than by turning again to an illustration from nature. There are three things necessary to the growth of a little child—namely, proper food, proper air, proper exercise. We will take this simple truth, and apply it in the spiritual realm, and the whole ground is covered. Grace is sufficient for spiritual growth.

What then are the means that we have to be careful concerning? First, the supply of proper sustenance to the life we have received. This is only to be found as we are fed day by day on the living Word. Second, the maintenance of a proper atmosphere in which our souls may grow and thrive. It is that of fellowship with God and His Son through the Holy Spirit. Third, the provision of proper exercise for the growing faculties and powers. This is obtained by the co-operation of the whole being with God in His enterprises in the world.

Let us take these things, and deal with them in the simplest way, for the sake of the youngest beginner in the Christian life. Have you life, my friend, my brother? Is that life maintained in health? Now you must observe the means of the grace in which you stand, in order to grow. You must first be a student of God's Holy Word. You must, secondly, live perpetually the life of prayer, which is the life of fellowship in the Spirit. Thirdly, you must be constantly about your Lord's work in the world. To neglect the study of the Word is to be unable to make progress toward the perfect likeness. To neglect the work of God is to find the powers, however carefully fed and atmosphered, becoming paralysed, and arrest placed upon development. Remember all these things are necessary. My final words here are not to be of exercise. That in itself is so important that I propose to deal with it later. My last words are to be about these two first things, the sustenance and the atmosphere of the life.

First, as to its sustenance. The reading of the Word of God? That is not enough. The study of the Word of God? That is still not enough. The answer of the life to the claim of the Word of God? That is the final thing I say to you with all solemnity, all carefulness and earnestness, if you will find me man, woman, or child who is neglecting the study of the Word of God, I will show you arrest of spiritual development. No other means to growth can take its place. You can no more develop Christian character by service without study of the Word and without prayer, than you can make the thundering locomotive run along the track unless you feed its fires. You cannot live by work in the physical realm unless you have proper food and air. This neglect—and God help me to say it kindly, even though it be a word of criticism—this has been the crying failure of the Christian Church.

Christian men and women in this age of busy fussiness have been, and still are, attempting to develop Christian growth by the things they do, while they neglect the culture of the life itself in the study of the Word of God, and response thereto. I beseech you, steep your spirit in its letter, and then its spirit shall dominate your spirit. Give time to study it diligently. Begin no day without some verse, or chapter, or book—I care not which. Quantity matters very little. The method matters everything. You say this is a busy age. I know it! I am in the age, and of the age. Do you have to be at business by a certain hour every morning? How often do you get there without your breakfast? Not often, of course. You cannot work without food. Will you care for the body, and not for the spirit? That neglect means arrest of development. It is absolutely important that you begin the day with God's Word. Man's words will be crowding upon your soul all day. Prepare it, then, with the Word of God, that you may measure and estimate rightly the words of men, accepting or rejecting them according to their relation with God's great Word. Feed your soul upon the Word. It is a means of grace.

But food is not sufficient. A man will soon be unable to take even the very best of food, if he remain in a house from which air is excluded. And so with the Word of God. You will soon cease to study it if you neglect prayer. You do not love your Bible as you used to do. There may be other reasons, but in all probability you have tried to study it as you would study Shakespeare or Milton, and you cannot do it. I can come to the great poets with the mind which God has given me, and by assiduous application I can catch some of their profound and mighty meanings. I cannot do that with my Bible. I can never open my Bible to write about it in exposition, or to teach it in the school, or to preach from it, without first lifting my heart to God, and casting my utter helplessness upon His wisdom and might. You must live the life of fellowship, the life of prayer. You must find time in the morning, and at noon, and at night, and in any case of need as the day passes over you, to lift your eyes to the height, and your heart to the throne, remembering that your High Priest is always with you; that your altar is erected in your

soul; that your place of worship is wherever
you are, on the mart, in the office, in the rail-
way train; on the mountain, or in the valley;
in the city or the village. Just where you are,
is the mercy-seat, and the Priest, and the altar,
and the place of prayer. We must cultivate
the habit of prayer if we are to live so as to
grow in grace. We must be men and women
of fellowship with God, of comradeship with
Jesus Christ; familiar enough to speak to Him
without preface or ending; breathing out to
Him the agony or the joy of the moment; telling Him everything as the day glides by.
Habits need to be created in the Christian life
as well as in the worldly life. A good habit
has to be cultivated, even as an evil habit. So
also with prayer. You must cultivate the habit
until presently it becomes second nature—no,
first nature—the principal business of your life
to tell Him everything, to speak with Him at
all times. You will tell Him your joys and
your sorrows. You will whisper your difficul-
ties, and along the highways, wherever you are,

you will commune with Him. Cultivate that habit of fellowship, and you will breathe the atmosphere of God's great mountain height. The man who would grow in grace—he is already grounded in that soil—must observe the means of grace, receive the sustenance of the Word, live in the atmosphere of prayer, and all the while he must exercise the life he has by co-operation in the enterprises of God.

Let me conclude by reverting to the standards already indicated. Are we more like Christ than we were? Let the question be asked by the soul of the Christian in the silent, secret place. Am I more like my Master than I was? Am I growing, or has there been somewhere an arrest in my development, so that I am less like Him than I was? If that be so, it is because of failure somewhere. Let us discover the cause of failure, and at all costs let us remove it, the disease of a year ago, or perhaps of twenty years ago. Go back to it, through the dead and dreary years in which you have lost your touch with God and Christ;

go back through the desolate darkness to the place where you parted company with your Lord, and there, though the journey bruise your feet, and wound your pride, and crucify your ambition, there cut out the things that have spoiled the Christ-life, and hindered your growth; and there you will know that His love is so graciously healing that all the scars will presently be obliterated. So masterfully and mightily run the tides of the Christ-life that He will give you back the years that the canker-worm has eaten, and restore to you all that your unfaithfulness has lost.

But if we can say, Yes, slowly, oh, so slowly, but surely, we are getting more like Him; then let us rest in the Lord, and wait patiently for Him, knowing that at last we shall see Him and be like Him, and even for us the perfection of consummation will be attained.

IV

WORK

"My Father worketh even until now, and I work."—
JOHN v. 17.

"Working together with Him."—2 COR. vi. 1.

THIS is now the fourth of this series of discourses on the simple things of the Christian life. Life, health, growth, work: that is the true order. It is impossible intelligently to speak of Christian work save as we have first considered the subjects mentioned. As in the material world, so also in the spiritual, death accomplishes nothing, disease weakens effort, dwarfhood is incompetent. To state that threefold principle from the positive side, life is always expressed in toil, health is the condition for victorious effort, and growth is increasing capacity for work.

We must tarry by way of introduction, to

emphasise the importance of these preliminary matters, for a great deal of the weakness and inefficiency of Christian service is due to the fact of their neglect. First, there can be no real work with God or for God unless there be in the soul the life of God. This may be stated in other ways, which perhaps to some will be more forceful. How can I persuade men to crown Him King, while I am still in rebellion against Him? How can it ever be possible for me to co-operate with Him in His work of bringing purity into human life, while I cherish impurity in my own heart? Or, to go back again to the figure which we are following in this series, how can a man who is dead co-operate with the living Lord?

That principle has been accepted and acted upon in certain departments of Christian activity, and neglected in others. For instance, I presume no one would think that any man was really fit to preach the Gospel of the Son of God who had not himself obeyed it. We should all be prepared to safeguard the pulpits of the Christian Church against the man who did not in his own heart and soul know the life of God. Here there is no difference of opinion; but we have not been quite so particular in other departments. We have not always been sufficiently careful in the matter of those appointed to teach in our Sunday Schools. The great essential in the instruction of children in the things of God is that their spiritual welfare should never be entrusted to one who knows nothing of spiritual life. Again, no persons should be put to lead the singing in a Christian church simply because they are musical. No man should touch the sacred work of the Christian faith at any point, save as he has received the life of God by the communication of the Spirit of God. To attempt Christian service in order to obtain life is utterly unreasonable and useless. Yet how often is this being done. How continually people come to those of us who are entrusted with oversight, and say they wish to take up some Christian work. And the first inquiry is, or ought to be, whether they belong to Christ. Sometimes the answer is given in the negative, and the hope is expressed that they will become His by working for Him. That can never be! In the name of God do not take up that work until you are born of God. For your own sake, for the sake of the work, for the sake of God, let none ever lay hands to Christian toil who is not a sharer of the Christ-life. Death, I repeat, can accomplish nothing.

To take the second point for emphasis. Our Christian service is always weakened when our spirituality is atrophied at any point. If there be no holiness of life, then service is always feeble. If I regard iniquity in my heart, even though I be a child of God, the Lord will not hear me; for if I thus put myself out of loving touch and fellowship with God, how can my service be accepted by Him, or be acceptable to Him? Herein is the heinousness of sin in the believer—sin permitted, excused, condoned—not merely that it injures the life of that particular soul, but that it paralyses the power of service. Every child of God is more than a treasure won for the heart of God. In His economy every child received is another soldier added to the ranks, another builder to help in rearing the great building. For battle and for building the Master came; and I can neither help Him in His fight, nor in His building, if my spiritual forces are weakened by the presence of anything in my life which is unholy, whether things of the flesh or of the mind, yea, even of the spirit. Does not this self-same apostle in this very connection urge us to "cleanse ourselves from all defilement of flesh and spirit, perfecting holiness in the fear of the Lord"? If there be an arrest in the spiritual development, there is also an arrest in the power for service.

This truth is so self-evident that it scarcely needs demonstrating. Here is a person who joined the Christian Church, shall we say, ten years ago? In those early days of Christian experience the vision was clear, and the love was intense and warm and passionate—"first love," as Jesus calls it. But gradually, through some evil thing permitted, the fire of enthusiasm has cooled, until hardly a spark is burning on the altar, and the old compassion has gone, until there is hardly any pitying love for the lost and undone. What is the inevitable result for the backslider as to his Christian service? He will either withdraw from it altogether, ceasing to offer the gift which he knows cannot be accepted, or he will maintain its outward form, observe its routine, and obey its ritual; but the constraining love, the personal devotion to his Lord and His interests, the peace and joy and blessing that he used to experience, are all wanting, and the service is lifeless and worthless. The arrest of development was at the same time arrest in the power of service. Consequently, I repeat, we can never intelligently speak of service save as we bear in mind the fact that there must first be life and health and growth.

If these things be granted, let me ask you to notice the Scriptures at the beginning of this study, as revealing the nature and power of Christian activity. Let us first take them separately and look at them in their relation to the context.

"My Father worketh until now, and I work." These words occur in connection with the story of the healing of the man who had been in the grip of infirmity for thirty-eight years. When Jesus had healed him, the rulers met and challenged him, demanding how he dared carry his bed on the Sabbath day. And the man, who did not know Jesus, did not know who He was, answered, with splendid artlessness and simplicity, "He that made me whole, the same said unto me, Take up thy bed and walk." Presently the rulers found Jesus, and sought to persecute Him, and to slay Him, because He had violated the Sabbath. It was in answer to that charge that our Lord thus spoke. To these critics of His action who were carping about the external, and had no sympathy with the deep, underlying meaning of love, He said, "My Father worketh until now, and I work." Will you let me put the inner meaning of that answer of Jesus into quite other words? It is as though He had said, God has no Sabbath, He has no rest. "My Father worketh even until now, and I work." It is as though He told them how man by his sin broke Sabbath for God, and how God can never find His rest until He has dealt with sin and put it away. "My Father worketh." There is fine irony in the answer, and splendid satire upon the pettiness of men who will let a crippled man lie unhealed in the porches rather than have the externality of the Sabbath violated. In effect, Jesus said to them as they criticised His action: I healed this man; it is My work, and My work is God's work, and We are both at work on the Sabbath because of sin. That man lying there in his infirmity is one of the evidences of the presence of sin in the world, and God cannot rest while man suffers as a result of his own sin. "My Father worketh even until now, and I work."

Thus we may deduce from this answer of Christ these meanings. It is His great declaration of the fact—and I pause for words, for to me it is one of the deepest and sublimest facts, and I hardly know how to express it— of God's restlessness in the presence of man's unrest. It is a sublime unveiling of the fact that God in His heaven cannot be at rest while the man He has made in His own image and likeness, the man who is His offspring by creation, is restless on account of sin. "My Father worketh even until now, and I work."

It is moreover, and therefore, a declaration of God's ceaseless activity toward the removal of the cause of man's unrest. What had Jesus done on that Sabbath day? Had He really broken the Sabbath? No, He had made Sabbath-keeping possible for a man. He had not broken in upon rest. He had created the opportunity for rest. He had not violated the great law that demands that man shall find opportunity for quietness and peace. Supposing Jesus had not passed that way on that

Sabbath day, or, passing, had passed on, and had left that man in his limitation, there would have been added to his tale of years another Sabbath without rest. How many he had had! Thirty-eight years, and perhaps in all of them no real Sabbath, nothing but pain and weariness, nothing but restlessness, nothing but the sickness of heart that comes from hope deferred; a poor, lone, bruised, broken man, without Sabbath. Jesus stands out as the revelation of God, as He says in effect, To give that man rest I lose My rest. To restore to him the living beauty of one golden Sabbath day I will heal him now and let him carry home his bed. He kept Sabbath that day. Every man knows that the activity of Jesus was activity toward the removal of the cause of human unrest. In Christ's activity I have a revelation of God's activity. Working, ever working, through processes which to our hurried, transient life seem very slow, but always working, restless in the presence of man's unrest, and for evermore striving toward the removal of the cause of man's unrest. That is God's work.

Then notice that Jesus brings Himself, in the simple affirmation of the text, and more wonderfully in the discourse which follows, into union with God in that work. "My Father worketh even until now, and I work." Jesus did not speak of a work which God had done, and which He then took up and carried on. He did not affirm that He continued God's work at a point where God left it. That would be misinterpretation of the words of Jesus. What He does affirm is His perfect unity with God. "My Father worketh even until now, and I work." We are both working. We are working in perfect co-operation. There is a splendid suggestion in that present tense of Jesus. He Who said of Himself, "I am," said of Himself, "I work." Not, I worked, or, I will work, or, I am working for the moment, but "I work." He declares His harmony with God. It is the co-ordination of toil which is here declared. God and Christ

are one in Their restlessness in the presence
of human unrest. They are one in Their
ceaseless activity to remove its cause.

Let us now turn to the phrase in the Corin-
thian epistle. I am not often given to taking
words out of their context, neither do I in-
tend to do so now in spirit. This phrase is
very suggestive. "Working together with
Him." The apostle has been defending and
explaining the Christian ministry; and incidentally and inferentially he gathers into his
great argument the thought of all such as are
in fellowship with God in life and service. If
you go back to the verses preceding you will
find that the apostle declares what God's work
is. "God was in Christ, reconciling the world
unto Himself." He then proceeds, "We are
ambassadors, therefore, on behalf of Christ,
as though God were entreating by us; we
beseech you on behalf of Christ, be ye recon-
ciled to God." "Working together with
Him." It is only a phrase; but it is lit with
glory, and charged with power. It declares

this man's realisation that he also is in the holy partnership, that he also has a share to take in the work of God. "My Father worketh even until now, and I work." "Working together with Him."

The work of the Christian man in the world begins with unceasing restlessness because of man's unrest. You are a Christian. Are you content in the world with the world as you see it? Tell me what you say when you look at evil, and I will tell you whether you are a Christ-man or not. Is there a Divine discontent burning in your heart, that drives you out into active service? Then you are working together with Him. Can you be perfectly at rest in this great city, with all its sin and sorrow and sighing and restlessness? Then you know nothing of His life in your soul. God cannot rest while men are restless. Can you?

This unrest expresses itself in unceasing conflict with sin. I thank God that He has never made peace with sin. I thank God that

He has never signed a truce with it in this poor heart of mine. How I have tried to persuade Him to! How, ever and anon in the years that have gone, I have tried to excuse some darling sin, but He has never made peace with it. I have known it, and have hidden it. I have had to say with the Psalmist, "When I kept silence, my bones waxed old through my roaring all the day long; for day and night Thy hand was heavy upon me." Thank God for His heavy hand wherever sin abides in the life. And so the man of God is filled with anger in the presence of sin. It is told of Hannibal that when he came in utter amazement and grief into the presence of his father, crucified by the Romans, he lifted his hand in the presence of that Roman cross, and swore by all his gods that he would fight to the death the power that had crucified his father. The Christian man is a man who has been to the Cross, and he has seen what sin has wrought for his God, and he lifts his hand in the presence of that Cross, and swears to fight sin to the death, in his own heart, in his home, in his city, in the world. My Father worketh against sin in ceaseless activity, and I work. We also are the sworn foes of sin, even as God is. Why is God the foe of sin? In order that He may save the sinner. I love that word *save*. Do not let us drop it out of our speech in these days. It is not a narrow word, shallow and meaningless. It is a great word. God is the foe of sin in order that He may save men. Why does God hate sin in me? Why has He never made peace with it? Because He knows that it harms me, and all the fiery fierceness of His wrath is fed by the fuel of His infinite love for the sinner. So, if we are workers together with Him, the purpose of our conflict with sin is that we may make Sabbath for the man who has none, that we may lead the restless into rest, the wounded into healing, the wearied home, and the lost back again to the heart of God.

Let us pass to the second thought, as to the power of Christian activity. "Working with

Him." "Working with" is one word in the Greek. The Greek preposition indicates the closest union possible. It is not one that can be translated "among," nor "by the side of." It must be translated "with," and even that "with" does not convey its full force. If we go back to Mark's Gospel (xvi. 20), where we have the picture of the disciples as they first went out to do the work which Christ had commanded them, we read, "the Lord working with them." It is exactly the same word as Paul uses when he says, "working together with Him." As the Lord wrought with them, so they wrought with the Lord. Mark the closeness of the union.

If this be so, see what it means for us who take up this sacred toil. Our toil is in the power of God. This power is always irresistible, and leads always to some issue. No man escapes it. It may issue in redemption or condemnation. The which depends wholly upon the response of the man who comes within its sphere. This message will be "a savour from

death unto death," or "a savour from life unto
life." Every message of God to men is a message of release or bondage, of salvation or
condemnation, of life or death. No man can
resist the power of God. If a man in his unutterable folly, instead of hiding in the heart
of God, fling himself against the strength of
His righteousness, he must inevitably work his
own destruction. No man can escape His
power.

Yet remember that while that is fearfully
true and never to be forgotten, it is also true
that the power of God is always beneficent in
intention, and is always acting toward the rec-
onciliation of man to Himself. "God was in
Christ reconciling the world to Himself."
Alienation from God will be through abuse of
the power that was intended for restoration.
The purpose of God is toward the reconcilia-
tion of man, and the healing of his wounds, and
the restoration of His Sabbath; and if any
should miss the way, and find himself at last
unreconciled, it will be of his own choice.

Doom and destruction will be by the power of God, but by the choice of man.

What, then, is our power as we work with God? Every piece of work done for God, by Christian souls in life and health, is God-energised. What is its purpose? The gathering of men back to God. What is its limitation? The measure of response in those among whom we work. I cannot compel any man to yield to God. God does not compel any man to yield to Him. He gives his will freedom of choice, which it never had until Jesus Christ came to create it for him. The man without Christ will have to say, "When I would do good, evil is present," and he is mastered. Jesus Christ comes with the dynamic of redemption, which is mightier than the forces which master man, so that now when he would do good he can say, "I can do all things in Him that strengtheneth me." Christ sets my will free for action. He never compels it to that action.

My young brothers in the Christian faith, I would to God that I might help you to see the glory of Christian service. There are some, perhaps, who are a little weary and tired. You teach in the Sunday School, and you wonder whether the toil and the drudgery are worth while. Lift your service and look at it in the light of these great words: "My Father worketh even until now, and I work." "Working together with Him." Therein is the glory of service, and except for that blessed assurance I think it could not be continued, but that the burden of it would crush out the very heart and life. But when I know that this little life of mine, with all its uncertainty of duration, in the comparative insignificance of its sphere, can yet be a life co-operative with God, then I am conscious of the dignity and the glory of my service, and I know that the weariness and the toil are abundantly worth while, and the scars of battle seem glorious. He was wounded. Then thank God for any wounding that has come to me in such service.

"Working together with Him." That is

the story of what you are doing, dear, tired heart. It is not just a class in the Sunday School. Do not speak of your work that way. Someone will meet you to-morrow, perhaps, and ask you what part you take in the church's work. Do not say that you only take a class. Say that you work with God. If you can so work through all the years as to get one child-heart and teach it to trust, you have done work that angels might envy. If I can make one Sabbath day for one broken heart, it is God's work, and Christ's work. Why should I want rest? Talk not to me of your Sabbaths. "My Father worketh," said Christ, "and I work"; and one apostle took up the word and said "working together with Him." You and I may be in the same great and gracious and glorious succession.

I return, in conclusion, to the things with which I commenced. The place of work in my personal life, what is it? I must have life. I cannot work with God unless I have the life of God. And growth ceases if toil ceases, just as toil will cease if growth ceases. These things are reflexive in their activity. To neglect service is to stop growth, to permit disease to destroy life ultimately. Dr. Alexander Maclaren once said in my hearing: "No man lighteth a candle, and putteth it under a bushel. But supposing he should put it under a bushel, what will happen? Either the bushel will put the light out, or the light will set the bushel on fire." That is the whole philosophy of the truths we have been studying.

Finally, what is the value of my work in the economy of God? Only by toil and travail can God's Kingdom come. God could not enter into the redeemed Kingdom but through the processes of redemption's passion. Christ could not take the kingdoms of the world by any other method than that of co-operation with His Father in the passion. He must tread the *via dolorosa* to its end. So, if I am to be a worker together with Him, I must also "bear in my body the marks of Jesus." I also must have wound-prints in my hands. I speak it solemnly. I speak it with a sense of shame at the easiness of my service. We have no part with Him until we suffer with Him. It is by travail that life begins. It is through passion that compassion becomes powerful.

And yet if it be true that *only* thus the Kingdom comes, it is also true that *surely* thus it comes. If the Cross is accomplished, then the crowning must issue. We are not fighting the central battle. We are simply doing the skirmishing of administration. Armageddon was won on Calvary. Think of it, dear heart, and remember it sometimes. The conflict is fierce enough to-day, but it is nothing in fierceness to that supreme hour in which God in Christ took hold upon the things that spoiled, and spoiled them; when He made a show of them openly, triumphing over them in it. By the cross the crown. By your suffering and your toil, something of His Kingdom. By co-operation with Him in the power of His might, and in fellowship with His suffering, something of the infinite glory. One of the old prophets, who saw far ahead, was singing of the victory that has not yet come, and as he sang, he borrowed the figure of motherhood to express the truth about God. It was Zephaniah, the man of fierce speech, and lightning denunciation, who suddenly merged into the sweetest song in the Old Testament. "He will rest in His love, He will joy over thee with singing." Mark it, God singing. Singing over what? Singing over a ransomed and redeemed people. He will rest one day. He will enter into perfect rest when He can sing over the perfect work of redemption. If I would enter into His rest and join in His song, I must enter into His travail, and have fellowship with Him in the day of His unrest and sorrow.

V

TEMPTATION

"One that hath been in all points tempted like as *we are*, yet without sin."—HEBREWS iv. 15.

IN this text certain words are italicised. They have been added for the sake of exposition. I propose to read, translating it quite literally, "In all, tempted after the likeness, apart from sin." The incompleteness of the words is at once recognised, and we are compelled, while considering them separately, to remember their vital connection with the statement immediately preceding them. "We have not a High Priest that cannot be touched with the feeling of our infirmities; but in all, tempted after the likeness, apart from sin." After declaring the sympathy of the High Priest Who has entered into the Holy Place, having passed through the heavens, the writer affirms that sympathy to be based upon the fact that He was "in all"—that is, in all our infirmities,—tempted "after the likeness"—in the same way—that is, after the same pattern, and yet with a radical difference, "apart from sin." Our text, therefore, suggests to us the identity of Jesus with us in our temptation—"tempted in all, after the likeness"; and His separation from us in that self-same temptation—"apart from sin."

Temptation is a common experience of man. The Christian man is more keenly conscious of its power than the man of the world. It often happens that in the experience of the soul newly yielded to Christ this fact causes great perplexity; and it may be well, by way of introduction, to say one or two words concerning it. Why is it, the young Christian, especially, often enquires, that since I yielded my life to Christ I have been more tempted than ever? The explanation always lies in the very fact of that surrender. Directly the human soul ranges itself on the side of Christ, it becomes peculiarly the object of enmity on the part of Satan and his emissaries. The devil is ever busy attempting to spoil God's fairest work, and to prevent the perfecting of the life received in the mystery of the new birth.

Another reason arises out of the very nature of the Christian life. With the new life there has come a new consciousness of evil, and a new sensitiveness in its presence. Temptation which came yesterday, but was hardly appreciated, comes again to-day, and is felt in all its force. It is well to remember this. The holier a man is, the more acutely conscious he is of temptation. The stronger a man is in all his moral fibre, the more does temptation appeal to him. It is not the weak man who feels the real force of temptation, for he yields resistlessly to it. It is not the impure man who suffers under temptation, for his moral fibres are no longer sensitive, and the suggestion of evil brings no pain. But the man in whom there has begun to move and thrill the pure, strong life of the Christ, the man whose spirit is dominated by the Holy Spirit, he it is who feels the full force and pain of temptation. That thing was temptation to me yesterday, ere I had met the Christ; but there was no pain in it, no strain, no tug, only a willing yielding. But when I yielded myself to Him, a new force came into my life, ennobling and purifying, and when temptation comes there is now resistance; my consciousness of it is keener, not only because the enemy is more earnest in his attack, but because my sensibility is greater. Let me say to the young child of God who is troubled by temptation, Take heart. Be of good courage. The man held fast in the grip of vice knows nothing of the pain of temptation. Take heart, and know that your sensitiveness to temptation is sure evidence of the new life, the new purity and power working dynamically through your personality.

This problem of temptation is constantly recurring. While much has been spoken and written concerning it, it is always, I think, of value to spend some time in facing the fact of its place and value in life. This cannot be better done than by careful study of the temptation of Jesus Christ, as the story is told in the Gospels, the fact of which is referred to by the writer of the letter to the Hebrews.

In that wilderness experience of Jesus there is first of all revealed to us quite incidentally, and yet with perfect clearness, the truth concerning the actual nature of man. Stripped of all accidentals, the Man of Nazareth is seen in stern conflict with temptation, and in the simplicity of the situation I see the Man in all the boldness and beauty of His essential manhood. In the next place, the spheres of our temptation are defined, for there are no avenues along which the enemy can possibly approach human personality save those revealed in the wilderness. He may vary the method of his coming. He may vary the day of his approach. He may come with a thousand different and differing stratagems. But the only ways in which he can finally storm the citadel are here declared. Then also the method of temptation is revealed. In each separate approach of the enemy the same underlying principle is discoverable. Finally, the method of victory is revealed.

First, then, in this story we have the revelation of human personality. Man is seen for what he really is. The order of the temptation indicates a line of development. The first temptation came through the physical, "Command that these stones become bread." The second temptation was directed against the spiritual, "If thou art the Son of God, cast Thyself down." Depend upon God. Trust Him. The third temptation made its appeal through the vocational, Behold the kingdoms of the world for which Thou hast come. Give me one moment's worship, and I will give Thee all Thy kingdoms.

Strenuously attempting to banish from our thinking the fact of temptation, let us now look at the Person presented to us. Man is in Him revealed as having a physical basis, as being spiritual in essence, and as existing for a specific purpose. Spiritual essence, a material basis, and an appointed work. This is the whole story of human life. Every human being has, as had this Man of Nazareth, a physical nature. The body is an instrument, "fearfully and wonderfully made," at once frail and enduring. Among all the inventions of science, nothing from any standpoint can compare with the human body; no machine ever conceived but has been patterned in some detail of its mechanism upon it, and yet by it is absolutely excelled. So delicate is it in its adjustment that "we fade as a leaf," and pass away with the wind. But that is only half the story. We are wont to compare the strength of the oak which has weathered the storms of a thousand years or more, with the weakness of the men who have sojourned under its shadow and died. I tell you that in the millennium which has passed over the head of the oak no storm has ever broken upon it equal to the storm that convulses a man in the hour of mental agony.

Then behind the physical, and superior to it, is man himself, the spiritual entity; man, using the eye of his body to see, the ear to hear, and the hand to feel. The spiritual fact is the supreme fact. Here in the wilderness I see a Man Who demonstrates in every onslaught of evil, the supremacy of the spiritual.

Again, the final fact is not that this being is created, but that he is created for purpose—in a word, that his whole *raison d'être* is accomplishment.

First, then, if I would understand aright my life in all its complexity of being, I must bring it back to, and place it beside, that of the Man of Nazareth; and there is no place in all His story where it seems to me I see more clearly and marvellously what humanity is than in that wilderness. The storm is sweeping over Him. The light is clear about Him. No loving voices break the silence. None but the one master foe is attacking Him. There in the rough, rugged, awful, lonely hour of temptation I see Him, and there I see myself in my essential nature. I am spirit, tabernacling within a temple of flesh, and moving in a material universe; and I am, in order that I may achieve that which God has appointed.

In the second place this wilderness experience declares to us the spheres of temptation. The first testing is in the physical realm, and is directed toward the spoiling of the instrument in its service of the spirit. "If Thou art the Son of God, command that these stones become bread." How innocent it looks. How natural it seems. Yet it is an attempt to ruin man, and prevent his final realisation of purpose by marring him through his material necessities.

Next the foe attempts to corrupt the spirit. Man's greatness is demonstrated by his privileges. He is the special object of God's love and protecting care. He is permitted fellowship with the Most High. The enemy tempted Him to trespass on His privileges, to presume on His greatness, and to trade on the Divine favour for the satisfaction of His spiritual pride and ambition. "If Thou be the Son of God, cast Thyself down." Experiment upon Thy relationship. So the enemy seeks to draw man away from God, and make him act, as it would seem, with great religiousness, and yet, in fact, with blasphemous self-will.

The enemy has still another mode of attack, and his final attempt is to spoil the realisation of purpose. Thou hast come for kingdoms. Take them at my hand. Take them as my gift.

In no case does the enemy suggest the abandonment of Divine intention. Bread? Every man has a right to bread. Trust in God? Every man should trust in God. Possess the kingdoms? Every man ought to possess his kingdoms. They are all perfectly right suggestions. We are not dealing with the method. I simply ask you to notice the avenues. Satan can reach man through the gratification of his physical being, through the corruption of his spiritual nature, and through the pollution of his methods in realising his vocation. All

temptations are exhausted in this revelation.
If it be possible for man to resist in the physical, and spiritual, and vocational, there is no
temptation left. The devil has no other avenue
of approach, no other method than these of
breaking in upon human personality, and spoiling it.

Now let us pass to the third line I suggested: the method of temptation, as revealed
in this wilderness story. It suggests the gaining of a right end by improper means. The
enemy dare not take away from man the only
vision strong enough to make him put forth
effort. He must leave the goal in view. The
pathway he suggests appears to go toward the
goal, but never reaches it. Here is the subtlety
of temptation: a proper thing to be gained by
improper methods. It is never done. No man
ever reaches the goal save along the straight
path thereto. Deviation is ultimate failure.

"Command that these stones become bread."
It is as though the devil said: You have been
placed in circumstances of hunger. This for

the moment is the arrangement of God for You. Break through it. You are hungry. It is perfectly right to be hungry, and it is perfectly right to make bread when God has not made it for You. It is perfectly right to satisfy a proper craving in Your life, even though You must act independently of law. Then, "It is written, He shall give His angels charge concerning Thee." Find out if that is true. Put God to the test. The moment you put God to the test by experiment, you prove, not that you trust Him, but that you do not trust Him. "Cast Thyself down." Do something heroic, splendid, great, spectacular. Reach the end of infinite repose upon the bosom of God, but reach the end by adventuring something. No, let Jesus name it: "By *tempting* the Lord thy God." Finally, Thou hast come for the kingdoms of the world. I do not suggest that Thou shouldest give up the hope of possession, that Thou shouldest turn Thy face from Thy goal. But see, the way marked out for Thee is one of suffering and contumely. Here is an easy method. One bending of the knee to me, and all the kingdoms are Thine. Thou hast come for kingdoms. I offer Thee what Thou hast come for, but by a short cut.

This is always the method of temptation. Where have you felt its force, say, this last week? Let the answer to that question be given in your own heart. But I declare this thing solemnly. You have felt the force of temptation through a desire which is right in itself, and the temptation has consisted in the suggestion that you should answer the right desire in the wrong way. That is the whole method of temptation. Bread there is the symbol of everything that answers the craving of the physical life. Whatever this flesh of mine desires, it ought to have, providing its satisfaction is in God's way. There is no essential power of my manhood that it profits me to crush, providing I can exercise it according to the provision and government of God. Evil is for ever saying, Here is a natural demand of your life. You want companionship, pleasure, amusement. Get it, get it anyhow. God has not given it to you, take it. That is the devil's suggestion. Know it for his whenever you hear it. He may not come to you as he came in mediæval times, according to the pictures of the great masters, with hoofs and horns. Marie Corelli was nearer the truth when she depicted his last appearance, in her book, on the threshold of the House of Commons. There is much philosophy in the suggestion. He will come to you in a thousand ways. He will come with siren voice and cultured demeanour, with infinite respectability of appearance. But if he tells you to answer the call of your nature at any cost, even though you are put where you cannot answer it according to the will of God, then know that voice for the voice of evil. No matter how he may be garbed, it is the devil. James Garfield said, "Men ought to dare to look the devil in the face and name him devil." We are a little afraid of talking of him to-day. But he is with us. We are perpetually talking of the lower instincts of our nature. There are no low instincts of your nature if you are a man. That which is low in your nature is the devil's presence there, prompting the misuse of the high instinct. That is temptation which is for evermore saying, Take this thing anyhow, if you cannot get it as you ought.

Again the temptation comes through man's spiritual prestige. Demonstrate your consciousness of God's favour. Tempt God. Be preeminently religious. Do some great thing to manifest your trust. Answer that deep craving of your life by some external manifestation. That is the voice of the devil.

Or, again, with regard to purpose in life. I have no sympathy, no patience with those who say the young should not be ambitious. They ought to dream dreams, and see visions, and climb mountains, and fight battles, and strive for success. God so made them. But the enemy comes and says: See, that is a rough and rugged road to the temple of fame. That is a hard and difficult hill. You will be long years toiling up it. Come with me, and I will show you a short cut. Know that voice for the devil's own. He is the prime inventor and patentee of short cuts. The man who would be rich by a short cut is devil-led, find him where you will. The man who would get his kingdom by half a moment's homage to some whispered evil suggestion of unrighteousness is devil-led. That is temptation, and its principle of appeal is always the same, the attaining of a right end by a wrong method.

Let us take the last of these thoughts. I pray you notice how wonderfully this wilderness story reveals the method of victory. How did this Man win when He was tempted? I am honestly more anxious that you shall see this last thing than anything else, because, though sublime, it is simple, and if we can get hold of this we can win. The appeal to the physical was withstood by an assertion that the care for the material life alone is a denial of the essential truth concerning man, and the spoiling of man's nature.

"Command that these stones become bread."
That is the devil's estimate that man's sole need
is bread. But listen to the answer, "Man shall
not live by bread alone." When you are
tempted in the realm of the physical, your answer is to be that the physical is not the only
thing, nor the most important, and the first
consideration must be the relationship between
the physical and the spiritual. Man does not
live only in the flesh. In his folly he may try
to. He may answer only the call of the flesh,
but in so doing there must inevitably be the
degradation of the spiritual. I take my watch
in my hand and for five minutes look at its
face, and on every moment is the impress of
eternity. There stands that loaf of bread. I
take it in my hunger when I ought not to have
it. What have I done? Taken a loaf of
bread? No! violated the law of the universe,
flung myself in all my unutterable folly athwart
the rhythmic march of God. "Man shall not
live by bread alone." I may have my half-
hour's physical satisfaction contrary to law,

but the infinite law enwraps me, fastens me, takes hold upon me. I cannot escape. If I can remember that, I shall not be likely to find answer to the call of the flesh, without asking how it will affect the spiritual, the eternal, the undying.

When the enemy proceeded further, and made his attack upon the spiritual, how then did this Man win? The appeal to the spiritual was refused by an assertion of the proper limits to the actions and attitudes of a dependent being. Trust God, said the devil. Trust God by experimenting. And the answer came, Such trusting is tempting. I can only trust God by trusting Him, and I can only trust Him by obeying Him, and I can only obey Him by waiting for Him. This is heroism. The suggestion of the devil was for heroism. If only you would do some great thing to prove your trust in God. If you could leap out from some height into immensity, relying upon the special exercise of God's providence, you would be heroic. It would be suicide? How can I be

your service. By one half-hour's homage you
have weakened your moral personality, spoiled
your ability to stand erect, and you will serve
the master to whom you yielded. Christ says
to the arch-enemy, I cannot worship, for that
would mean serving. I will worship God and
serve Him. So He chose God's way to the
Kingdom, even though it was the way of the
Cross, and the way of suffering.

In conclusion, let me ask you to notice this
fact. In the temptation of Jesus we have seen
the testing of absolutely perfect Man. I need
not stay to argue that. The sinlessness of
Jesus is admitted. I have been looking at the
temptation to sin of Him in Whom was no
sin. And so we read that He was tempted
"apart from sin," meaning not merely that He
did not sin by yielding, but that there was no
sin in His nature that could answer to temptation; no sin working within Him like a fire and
a poison, rendering Him liable to attack.
There was no weakening of the moral fibre of
Jesus through either inherited or contracted

sin. It was a perfect Man Who met temptation in the wilderness.

In a moment you tell me, and rightly, that there in that fact of His sinlessness, is the supreme difference between Jesus and all other men. You say, Is it true that He was tempted in all points like as I am? Did He know my experience of pain and struggle in the presence of evil? The Bible answers, "tempted in all points like as we, sin apart." Then you say, How does that help me? How does this whole study help me? What is the use of telling me that I am to resist as He resisted, if I cannot begin where He began? For it is true that no man can begin where He began. Account for it as you will; use what terminology you choose; there are within his very personality fires and forces and poisons. Call it tendency to sin, bias to evil, original sin; the fact is there, and Paul expressed it when he said, "The good which I would, I do not: but the evil which I would not, that I practise."

You ask again, How can I imitate Him?

You cannot imitate Him. We cannot win as He won. We cannot resist temptation as He resisted. Our moral fibre is weakened by our own past sin, for I care to say nothing about tendencies inherited. I come into the place where the devil appeals to my physical life, and try to insist upon its right relation to the spiritual, and I fail while I try. What shall I do?

This great text began by speaking of a High Priest. In that word Priest there is suggestiveness of other facts in the ministry of Jesus which must be taken into account, which we have already considered in another connection. How am I to resist? asks a man, looking at me with wild and hungry eyes, as he feels the force of a temptation. Hand yourself over to Jesus Christ in definite surrender. His Holy Spirit will come into your life, and take possession of it, and hold its citadel against the forces of evil. As Christ conquered sin, so the Christ-indwelt man may conquer sin. You have but to put your whole being under the control of

Christ, that you may receive from Him the Divine life, and realise the Divine strength, knowing that behind your own enfeebled activity there will operate the matchless and measureless might of God in Christ. No man can resist temptation by imitating Christ. He must be a Christ-indwelt man.

Any man and every man can be Christ-indwelt now if he will. The only way is that he take his life, weakened in its moral fibre by past sin, not strong enough in its own strength to resist, and hand it over to Him. Those who have read Bunyan's "Holy War" will remember how the citadel of Mansoul is at length possessed by Emanuel, and thus is held against the foe. As in the allegory, so in reality. Let Emanuel occupy your citadel, and in the hour of assault hand over the battle to your Lord. Make use of Him, the Indwelling One. Remit to Him the onslaught of the foe. Our text is immediately followed by the exhortation, "Let us therefore draw near with boldness unto the throne of grace, that we may receive mercy,

and may find grace to help in time of need."
I am never tired of pointing out that the Greek
phrase there translated, "in time of need," is a
colloquialism, of which the "nick of time" is
the exact equivalent. "That we may have
grace to help in 'the nick of time.'" Grace
just when and where I need it. Your life
is remitted to Jesus. You are attacked
by temptation, and at the moment of assault
you look to Him, and the grace is there
to help in "the nick of time." No postpone-
ment of your prayer till Sabbath. No post-
ponement of your petition until the evening
hour of prayer; but there, man, there in the
city street with the flaming temptation in front
of you, turn to Christ within you, with a cry
for help, and the grace will be there in "the
nick of time."

We have seen the processes of temptation
and the method of victory. We know our
weakness, but thank God for One Who met and
mastered temptation, "sin apart." He now, by
the mystery of His passion and dying, comes

into our lives, in us and through us to win as He won in the loneliness of the days long gone by.

May God help us to depend upon Him alone.